Weather Report

Bob Chilcott

for SSAATTBB unaccompanied

Composer's note

Weather Report was written for Stephen Cleobury and the BBC Singers as a programme ender for their concert tour of Japan in the summer of 2005. I wanted to write a piece that combined an ensemble virtuosity with a vocal jazz idiom—in fact the very kind of idiom that I was familiar with as both a singer and arranger when I sang with the King's Singers. This kind of style requires most importantly a great sense of vocal unity, of rhythmic and harmonic integrity, and a sense of style and shape that will hopefully give wings to the lyrics—lyrics that emphasize in the most charming and silly way the English obsession with the weather.

Duration: *c.*5 minutes

MUSIC DEPARTMENT

OXFORD
UNIVERSITY PRESS

OXFORD
UNIVERSITY PRESS

Great Clarendon Street, Oxford OX2 6DP, England
198 Madison Avenue, New York, NY 10016, USA

Oxford University Press is a department of the University of Oxford.
It furthers the University's aim of excellence in research, scholarship,
and education by publishing worldwide in

Oxford New York
Auckland Cape Town Hong Kong Karachi
Kuala Lumpur Madrid Melbourne Mexico City Nairobi
New Delhi Shanghai Taipei Toronto

With offices in

Argentina Austria Brazil Chile Czech Republic France Greece
Guatemala Hungary Italy Japan Poland Portugal Singapore
South Korea Switzerland Thailand Turkey Ukraine Vietnam

Oxford is a registered trade mark of Oxford University Press
in the UK and in certain other countries

12

ISBN 978-0-19-335644-3

Music origination by
Enigma Music Production Services, Amersham, Bucks.
Printed in Great Britain on acid-free paper by
Caligraving Ltd, Thetford, Norfolk.

for Stephen Cleobury and the BBC Singers,
for their tour of Japan, July 2005

Weather Report

Traditional rhymes

BOB CHILCOTT

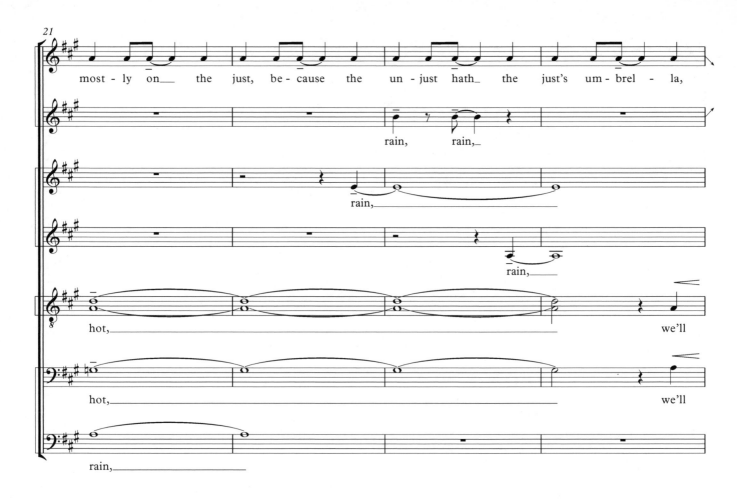

8

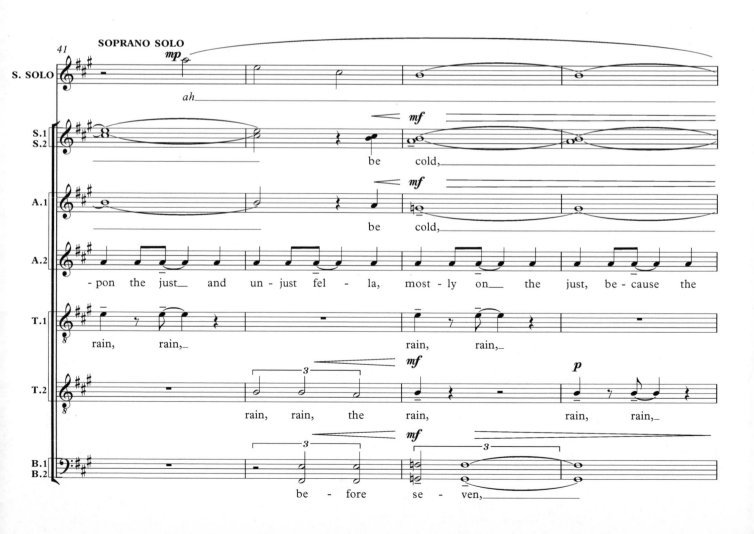

Steady and a bit sleazy

♩ = *c.*96 **(Tempo II)**